PEEL + DISCOVER®

HORSES

Welcome to your Peel + Discover activity book!

Inside are **hundreds of stickers** of horses. You'll find everything you need to care for them, train them, and ride them.

But this is a sticker book unlike any other! As you learn about ponies, palominos, and pole bending, you can sticker, draw, and add your ideas to make a book that's all your own.

LET'S GO FOR A RIDE! →

Library of Congress Cataloging-in-Publication Data is available.
ISBN 978-1-5235-0360-5

Workman books are available at special discounts when purchased in bulk for premiums and sales promotions as well as for fundraising or educational use. Special editions or book excerpts can also be created to specification. For details, contact the Special Sales Director at the address below, or send an email to specialmarkets@workman.com.

Workman Publishing Co., Inc.
225 Varick Street, New York, NY 10014-4381
workman.com

WORKMAN and PEEL + DISCOVER are registered trademarks of Workman Publishing Co., Inc.

Printed in China
First printing December 2018
10 9 8 7 6 5 4 3 2

PHOTO CREDITS: Courtesy of Emily Unger, p. 16 (bottom page): horseback riders in forest. age fotostock: Sara Landvogt, p. 4 (bottom page): Morgan horse; Tierfotoagentur/R. Richter, p. 4 (sticker): Running Morgan horse. Alamy Images: Mar Photographics, p. 4 (bottom page): Clydesdale horse in harness. Dreamstime: Songquan Deng, p. 24 (bottom page): Policeman on horse; Julie Feinstein, p. 24 (sticker): Policeman on horse; Rhbabiak13, p. 24 (bottom page): Horses pulling plow; Lukas Gojda, pp. 16 and 24 (sticker): Race horses with jockeys; Afif Abd Halim, p. 24 (bottom page): Polo players on horses; Martin Hatch, p. 16 (sticker and bottom page): Tent pegging; Stefan Holm, p. 24 (sticker and bottom page): Drum horses; Jdazuelos, p. 24 (sticker): Male polo player; Danny Raustadt, p. 20 (bottom page): Rodeo barrel racing; Olga Rudneva, p. 16 (sticker and bottom page): Jockey on horse; Tanya Yurkovska, pp. 4 and 24 (bottom page): Jockey on horse. Getty Images: 26ISO/E+ p. 20 (sticker): cactus; Gary Alvis, pp. 8 and 20 (sticker and bottom page): Saddle, cowboy boots; CasarsaGuru, p. 8 (bottom page): Hoof cleaning; DNY59, p. 8 (sticker): Cowboy boot; GH01, p. 20 (sticker): Boot spurs; GlobalP/iStock, p. 20 (sticker): Armadillo; ithinksky/E+, p. 20 (sticker): Cactus; Kerrick, p. 24 (sticker): Frisian horse; Silke Klewitz-Seemann, p. 4 (bottom page): Holsteiner horse; Ambramova_Kseniya, p. 3; Liliboas, p. 20 (sticker): Cowboy hat; olgaT, p. 4 (sticker): White stallion, Lusitano stallion. All additional images: Adobe Stock, Dreamstime, Shutterstock.com, Vector Stock.

saddle up!

Riding Journal

Rider Name: _____

Horse Name: _____

There are more than 58 million horses in the world.

RACING DERBY
seat 20
section 10
AUG 09

...NG DERBY
seat 21
section 10
AUG 09

Draw yourself riding a horse.

People have been riding horses for thousands of years!

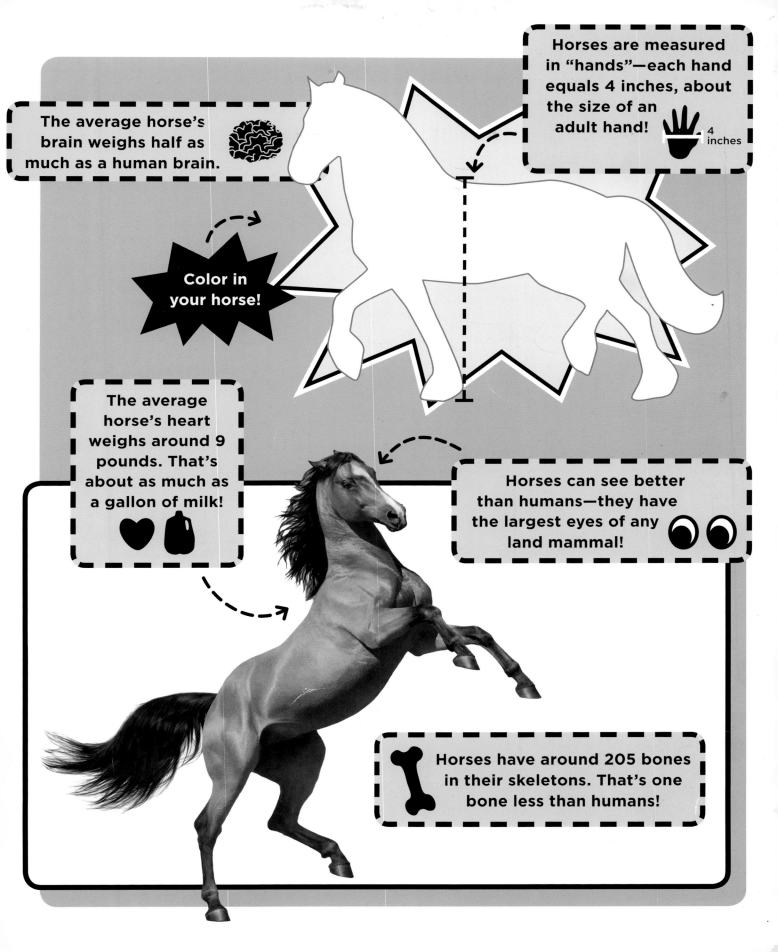

The average horse's brain weighs half as much as a human brain.

Horses are measured in "hands"—each hand equals 4 inches, about the size of an adult hand!

4 inches

Color in your horse!

The average horse's heart weighs around 9 pounds. That's about as much as a gallon of milk!

Horses can see better than humans—they have the largest eyes of any land mammal!

Horses have around 205 bones in their skeletons. That's one bone less than humans!

What was the Clydesdale bred to haul?

Blood Type

Horses are called cold-blooded, warm-blooded, or hot-blooded not because of the temperature of their actual blood.

What is the only horse breed named after a singer?

The Morgan is named after Justin Morgan, a traveling singer who received the first Morgan as a gift in 1789.

How can you identify a Holsteiner?

Which horses were originally Spanish war horses?

How can you spot an Appaloosa?

You can identify an Appaloosa by its spotted coat. These horses can have various patterns—leopard, snowflake, frosted, marble, and more!

How did the Quarter Horse get its name?

The American Quarter Horse was the first racehorse in America! It was named because its short, fast legs helped it sprint for the first quarter mile of a race.

What is the fastest breed of horse?

Thoroughbreds are the fastest horses, with a speed record of over 43 miles per hour! The fastest human sprinter's record is only 28 miles per hour.

43 mph

28 mph

Why do Arabian horses have black skin?

Arabians are originally from a hot desert climate. So, under their hair they have black skin to protect them from the sun!

Peel me up!

horse breeds

There are about 400 different **breeds**, or types, of horses!

Sticker and draw to fill your stable.

art marks

Some horses have whorls on their faces—these are swirls of hair, just like a cowlick!

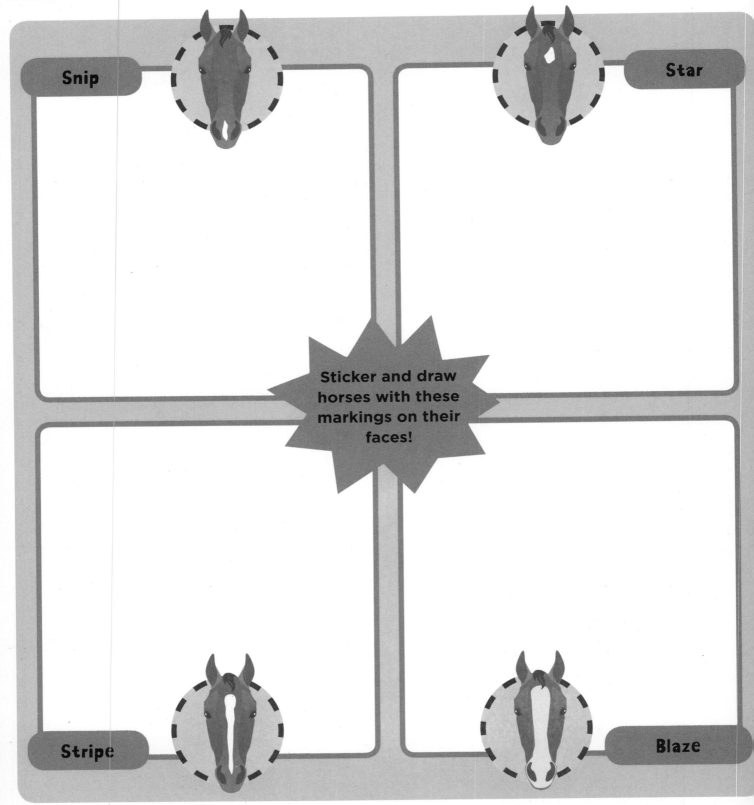

Snip

Star

Sticker and draw horses with these markings on their faces!

Stripe

Blaze

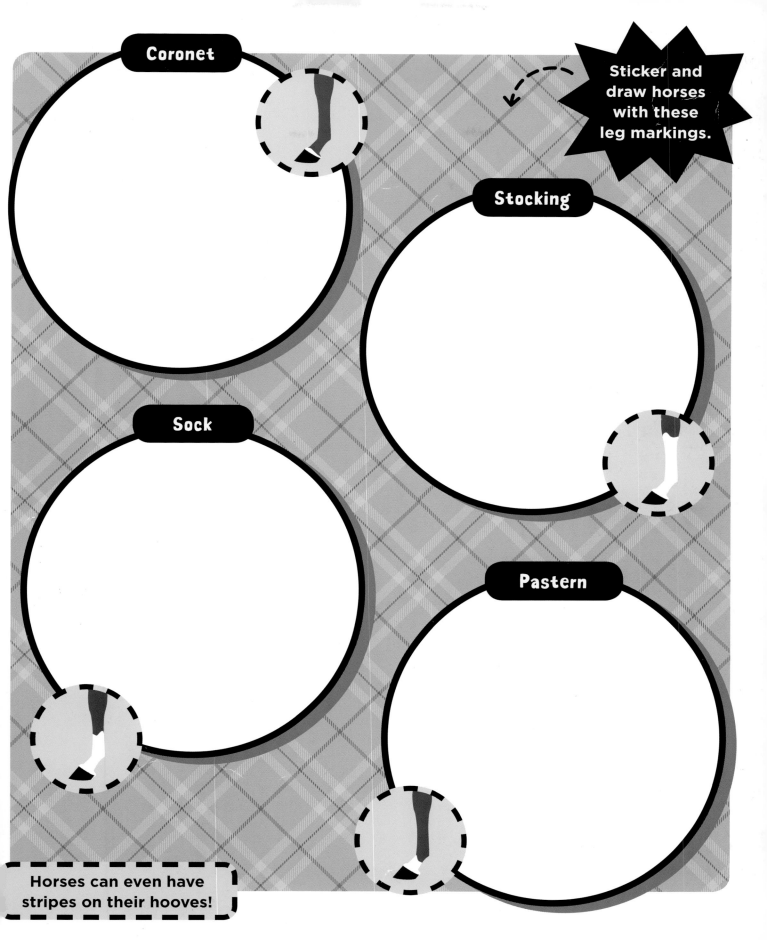

Coronet

Stocking

Sock

Pastern

Sticker and draw horses with these leg markings.

Horses can even have stripes on their hooves!

What do horses eat?

Horses have vegetarian diets based on their size and job. They can eat corn, grass, straw, oats, salt—even sugar beets and treats like apples and carrots.

How much water does a horse drink per day?

What are the two most common types of saddles?

How does a horse sleep in its stall?

Poll

Crest

Muzzle

Loins

Parts of a

Hock

How did the curry comb get its name?

Horseshoes were invented to protect a horse's hooves, which are made of keratin. That's the same material as your fingernails!

Why do horses wear shoes?

What is a hoof pick used for?

↑ Peel me up!

horse care

Sticker and draw to fill your barn with what you need to care for your horse.

Too many sugary treats can make a horse rowdy—like a sugar high! The sugar in foods like molasses and corn can make a horse buck more.

Horses with light skin need shelter on sunny days or they can get a sunburn!

ready to ride

Tack is the equipment a horse needs to do its job—like a saddle and a bridle.

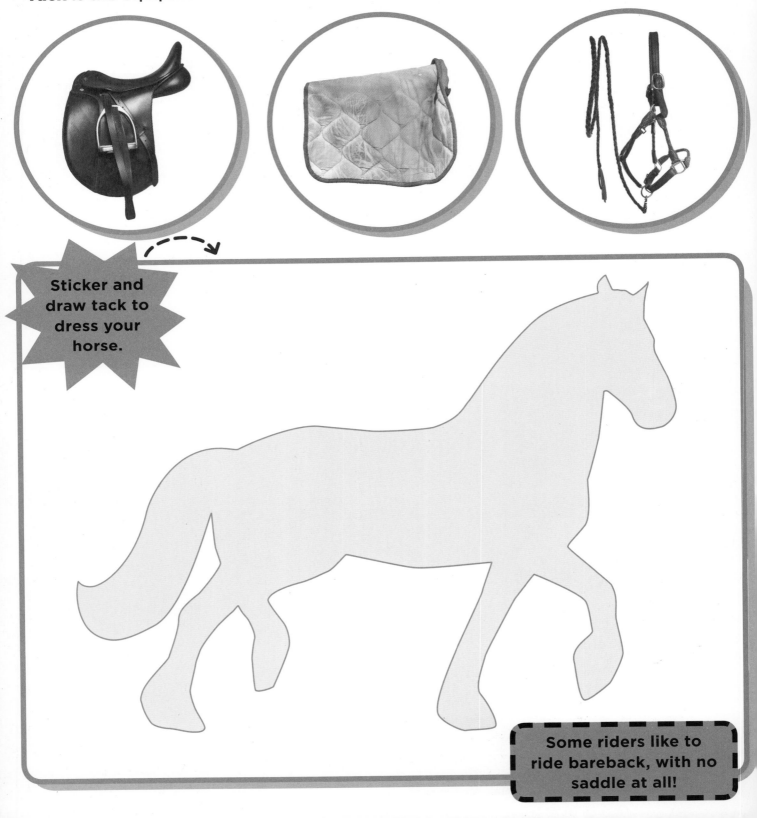

Sticker and draw tack to dress your horse.

Some riders like to ride bareback, with no saddle at all!

horse care

Sticker and draw to fill your barn with what you need to care for your horse.

Too many sugary treats can make a horse rowdy—like a sugar high! The sugar in foods like molasses and corn can make a horse buck more.

Horses with light skin need shelter on sunny days or they can get a sunburn!

ready to ride

Tack is the equipment a horse needs to do its job—like a saddle and a bridle.

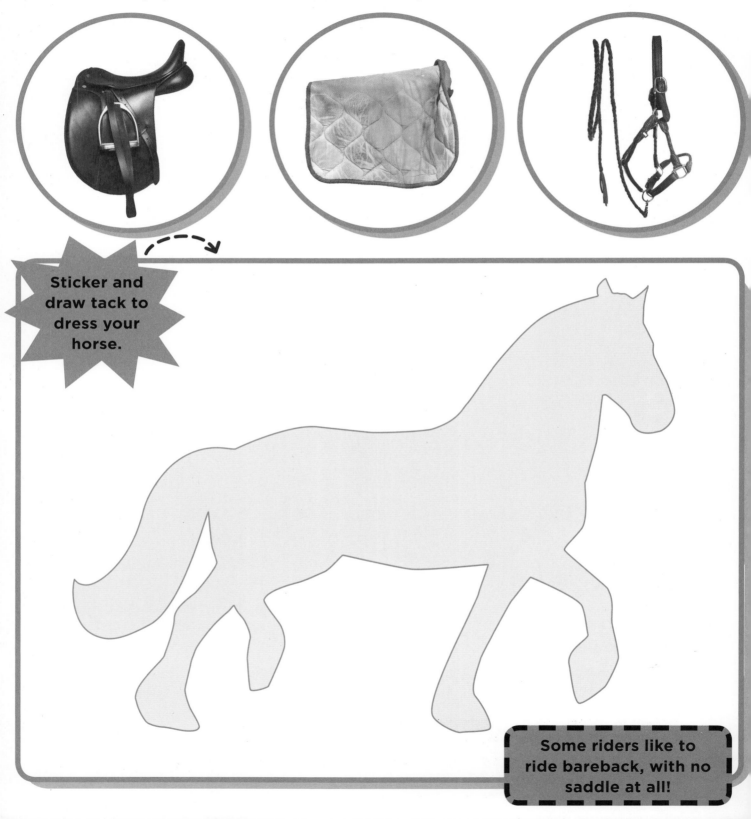

Sticker and draw tack to dress your horse.

Some riders like to ride bareback, with no saddle at all!

Draw yourself. Then sticker and draw to add the gear you need to go for a ride!

Life Cycle of a Horse

Foal
Birth to 1 year old

Colt
Birth

Adult Horse

When can you start riding a horse?

When a horse has been trained to wear a saddle and carry a rider, it is called "saddle broken." Many horses are saddle broken at age 2.

What do Shetland ponies eat?

When do foals take their first drink of milk?

How can you tell how tall a new horse will be?

At birth, a foal's legs are 80 to 90% as tall as they will be when they're fully grown!

Stallions and geldings are male horses. Males mostly have 40 teeth, while females usually have less!

What color is a palomino foal?

Palomino horses are known for their golden coats. But the foals can be born peach, cream, or beige. Their color changes as they get older!

How many teeth do foals have?

A young horse is called a foal. Foals are born with no teeth, but usually have 4 chompers by the end of the first week!

Peel me up!

baby horses

A **filly** is a young female horse. A **colt** is a young male horse.

Foals can nap, nurse, gallop, and even jump.

Sticker and draw fillies and colts at play.

Most foals are born at night!

growing up

Lead training begins by putting a halter on a horse. It helps young horses get used to being around people and taking directions.

Sticker and draw to add halters and saddles to the horses. Then add other horses in training!

Saddle breaking trains a horse to wear a saddle and carry a person's weight.

Young horses often live with their mothers or in herds.
Horses are happier and more secure living together.

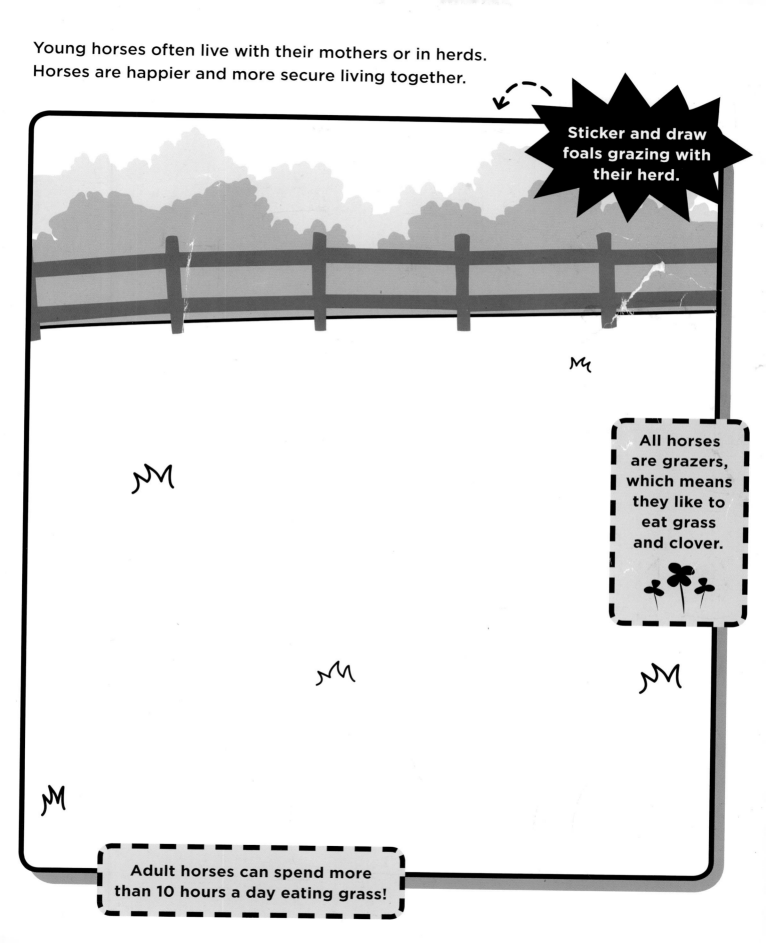

Sticker and draw foals grazing with their herd.

All horses are grazers, which means they like to eat grass and clover.

Adult horses can spend more than 10 hours a day eating grass!

In what sport do riders use swords?

In a tent pegging competition, riders use a sword to pick up and carry small pegs made of cardboard or wood!

In cross-country jumping, riders and their horses jump over obstacles like logs, trees, ditches, and streams.

In which competitive event do horses jump over logs and even streams?

Which riders sometimes need headlamps?

Let's Go to the Show!

Trails and Fields
Cross-country jumping
Tent pegging
Endurance riding

Indoor Arena
Show jumping
Horseball
Equestrian vaulting
Dressage

Outdoor Arena
Show jumping
Dressage
Tent pegging
Horseball
Equestrian vaulting

Horse Track
Tent pegging
Horse racing

How long has dressage been an Olympic sport?

Dressage has been an Olympic sport for more than a hundred years! Riders guide horses through a series of movements—like pirouettes and flying changes.

How do you find out a racehorse's birthday?

In horse racing, all horses are given the same birthday—January 1! This makes it easier to group the horses that are born in the same year for races.

In what sport are the riders sometimes upside down?

Jokers, hogsbacks, and oxers are types of fences in show jumping. A horse and rider must jump over each carefully—some are 6 feet high!

6 feet

In which sport do horses jump over jokers, hogsbacks, and oxers?

How do riders catch and throw a horseball?

Peel me up!

english riding

In an **endurance race,** horses and their riders race for long distances—sometimes the races last several days! In these races, horses must stop at checkpoints for food, water, rest, and checkups.

Sticker and draw flags to mark the trail, then add horses!

CHECKPOINT

FINISH!

Sticker and draw what you'd use to take care of your horse at this checkpoint.

jumping to win

In a horse show, horses of all different breeds compete in different **classes**, or events, for awards.

Sticker and draw to set up the arena for a horse show.

Show jumping is an Olympic sport!

HORSE SHOW

Show jumps are often colorful and creative, to test a horse's courage.

Sticker and draw to make your own show jumps.

You've won! Sticker and draw your award and winning horse.

What were the first cowboy hats made out of?

What is the fastest event in a rodeo?

What is a piggin string?

What does it mean to "tack up" a horse?

Team Roping

Calf Roping

What is a pole horse?

A pole horse performs in a pole bending race. But the poles don't actually bend— the horse has to bend its body around each pole as it weaves between them!

In barrel racing, a horse and rider race around 3 barrels. The first is called the money barrel because riders can often win money if they win the race! $

What is a money barrel?

Is the rider or the horse judged in a bronc riding event?

Peel me up!

western riding

Sticker and draw the western tack you need to get your horse ready for a trail ride.

Draw on the map where you'd like to go for a ride!

Trail Map

let's go, rodeo!

At a rodeo, cowboys, cowgirls, and their horses compete in events that test their skills and speed.

Sticker and draw what you need for the rodeo!

When a rider is thrown off a bucking horse it's called "biting the dust!"

Sticker and draw rodeo events.

The sport of calf roping began as a ranch skill—cowboys needed to quickly rope sick or injured calves to help them get treatment.

How can horses help people to learn, grow, and heal?

Some horses work as therapy horses. People not only ride them, but they also spend time with them, groom them, and care for them!

What does a cow horse do?

What does a draft horse do?

How long have horses pulled carriages?

What kind of training does a police horse need?

What is a jockey's job?

Oldest breed: Arabians

4,500 years old

Strongest type: Draft horses

How many drums does a drum horse carry?

Tallest breed: Shires

86 inches

How long have horses been used to play polo?

Peel me up!

working horses

Racehorse

Police horse

Sticker and draw to add the horses for each job.

Draft horse

Cow horse

Draft horses are big animals—each day they can eat twice what other horses eat!

my favorite horse

Sticker and draw yourself with your horse.

The name I would give my favorite horse is _____.

This horse loves to _____.

The best thing about this horse is _____

_____.